W9-AOY-981

CAMOUFLAGE
Survival in the Wild

Kennon O'Mara

The Rosen Publishing Group's
PowerKids Press™
New York

Published in 2009 by The Rosen Publishing Group, Inc.
29 East 21st Street, New York, NY 10010

Book Design: Daniel Hosek

Photo Credits: Cover © Phil Morley/Shutterstock; p. 5 © Michael Klenetsky/Shutterstock; p. 5 (inset) © Cora Reed/Shutterstock; pp. 6, 8, 9, 16, 19, 21, 22 courtesy Wikimedia Commons; p. 7 © Styve Reineck/Shutterstock; pp. 10–11 © Tony Wear/Shutterstock; p. 12 © Al Parker Photography/Shutterstock; p. 13 © Eric and David Hosking/Corbis; p. 14 © Larsek/Shutterstock; p. 17 © Barbara Tripp/Shutterstock; pp. 18, 20 © Ra'id Khalil/Shutterstock; p. 23 © Ron Hilton/Shutterstock; pp. 24–25 © Keith Levit/ Shutterstock; p. 26 (arctic hare) © National Geographic/Getty Images; p. 26 (arctic fox) © CoverStock/ Shutterstock; p. 27 © Gail Johnson/Shutterstock; p. 28 © Robert Hardholt/Shutterstock; p. 29 © Gary & Sandy Wales/Shutterstock.

Library of Congress Cataloging-in-Publication Data

O'Mara, Kennon.
  Camouflage : survival in the wild / Kennon O'Mara.
      p. cm. — (Real life readers)
  Includes index.
  ISBN: 978-1-4358-0153-0
  6-pack ISBN: 978-1-4358-0154-7
  ISBN 978-1-4358-2985-5 (library binding)
  1. Camouflage (Biology)—Juvenile literature. I. Title.
  QL767.O56 2009
  591.47'2—dc22
                                        2008036799

Manufactured in the United States of America

Contents

Blending In

Have you ever been surprised by an animal hidden in nature? Have you ever wondered why animals are certain colors? Many animals have camouflage (KAA-muh-flahj) that helps them **survive** in the wild.

Many animals are born with camouflage. Some animals have coloring that blends in with their **environment**. Others look or act like different animals or objects in their environment. Some can change as their environment changes. Camouflage helps animals hide from **predators** or catch prey. Let's take a look at some of the best examples of camouflage in nature.

WHAT IT IS
- the ways that animals blend in with their surroundings

MORE ABOUT IT
- camouflage can be the color or shape of an animal's body
- camouflage can be how an animal acts

CAMOUFLAGE

EXAMPLES
- green lizard hiding in green leaves
- butterfly that looks like another kind of butterfly that tastes bad to birds
- harmless snake that makes sounds like a deadly snake

NOT EXAMPLES
- green lizard hiding under a grey roc
- butterfly that eats things to make it taste bad to birds
- deadly snake that makes sounds to scare enemies away

You've probably seen people in camouflage clothing. People and animals have many reasons for blending into their environments.

Underwater Camouflage

Many sea animals have camouflage. The **reef** stonefish resembles the stone or coral in its environment. It's brown or grey with patches of color. It usually lives near the sea floor and sometimes buries itself in sand or mud.

The stonefish's camouflage helps it catch its food. Fish and **crustaceans** don't notice it until it's too late. The stonefish uses its amazing speed to grab prey. It's so fast that people need a special camera to see it move!

The reef stonefish has another **adaptation** to protect it. The fin on its back contains a poison that can kill other animals and even people!

Do you see the reef stonefish?

The reef stonefish can be found in the Indian and Pacific oceans.

These nudibranchs are called clown nudibranchs.
They get their bright colors from their food.

Another sea creature that uses color to hide itself is a sea **slug** called the nudibranch (NOO-duh-brank). Over 3,000 kinds of nudibranchs live in oceans in many parts of the world.

This small animal eats sponges and other ocean animals. Sponges get their color from **pigment** in their food. When some nudibranchs eat sponges, the pigment changes their skin color, too. This makes a nudibranch almost invisible on a sponge of the same color. It can eat while hiding from other animals. The nudibranch changes color when it eats a sponge with a different-colored pigment.

If its camouflage doesn't protect it, a nudibranch can release a liquid through its skin that tastes bad to other animals.

The leafy sea dragon is a fish with skin flaps that resemble leaves. It got its name from its long **snout** and neck that make it look like a tiny dragon. The leafy sea dragon usually has brown, yellow, or green coloring and may grow to be 18 inches (46 cm) long.

Leafy sea dragons have fins to help them move, but they mostly float slowly through the water like a piece of seaweed. This adaptation helps sea dragons hide from enemies and surprise prey. Fish that might eat leafy sea dragons think they're seaweed. The animals that leafy sea dragons eat, such as **plankton** and small crustaceans, don't notice them until it's

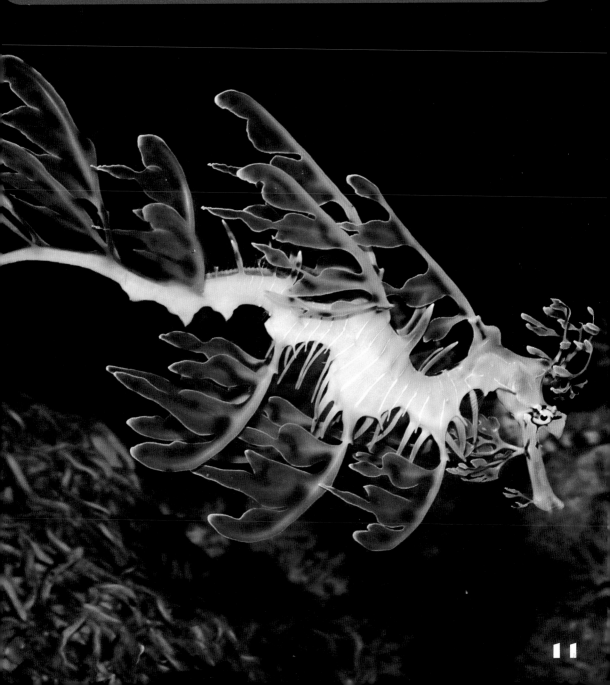

11

Camouflage with Wings

Many kinds of birds have camouflage. The ruffed grouse has a small crest of feathers on its head and a fanlike tail. Its feathers are grey, brown, white, and black. These colors blend in with leaves, dirt, and branches on the ground.

Ruffed grouse need to blend in because they nest on the ground, rather than high up in trees like many other birds. They eat leaves, berries, seeds, and insects on the ground. The female depends on her camouflage for protection from predators while she sits on the nest.

In winter, ruffed grouse hide in mounds of snow. They grow more feathers to keep them warm. Also, their feet adapt so they can walk on the snow, just as if they were wearing snowshoes!

Ruffed grouse are found in the forests of Canada and the northern and eastern United States.

The American bittern eats frogs, fish, insects, mice, and other small animals found in wetlands.

The American bittern is found around **wetlands**. It spends winters in the southern United States and Central America and summers in the United States and Canada.

The American bittern has a mostly brown body with dark and white spots that help it hide in patterns of light and shadow. When it senses danger, it stands still and points its bill up. Its thin head and neck resemble the surrounding reeds and grasses. The bittern's predators may not see it among the plants. This behavior also helps it surprise prey. The bittern usually hunts around sundown, when it's harder for other animals to see it.

Two Camouflaged Birds

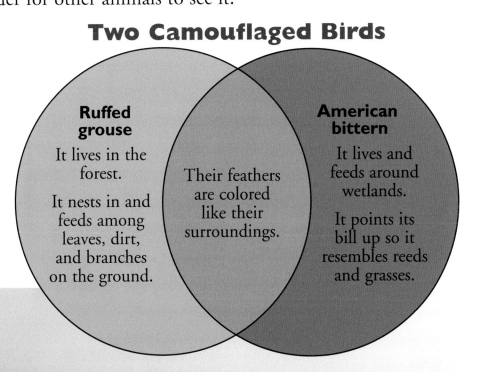

Ruffed grouse

It lives in the forest.

It nests in and feeds among leaves, dirt, and branches on the ground.

Their feathers are colored like their surroundings.

American bittern

It lives and feeds around wetlands.

It points its bill up so it resembles reeds and grasses.

Insect Camouflage

Many butterflies have wings that resemble brightly colored leaves or dead, brown leaves. When these butterflies are at rest, predators often think they're leaves.

The owl butterfly of Central and South America is mostly brown with black markings, which helps it blend in with tree bark. It also has a large circle on each wing. The circles resemble an owl's eyes. These markings may scare off animals that like to eat butterflies, such as birds and lizards.

Owl butterflies are large and don't fly very far, so they're easy to see and catch when moving. Some scientists think predators attack the "eyes" on the butterfly's wings, which protects its body from harm until it can get away.

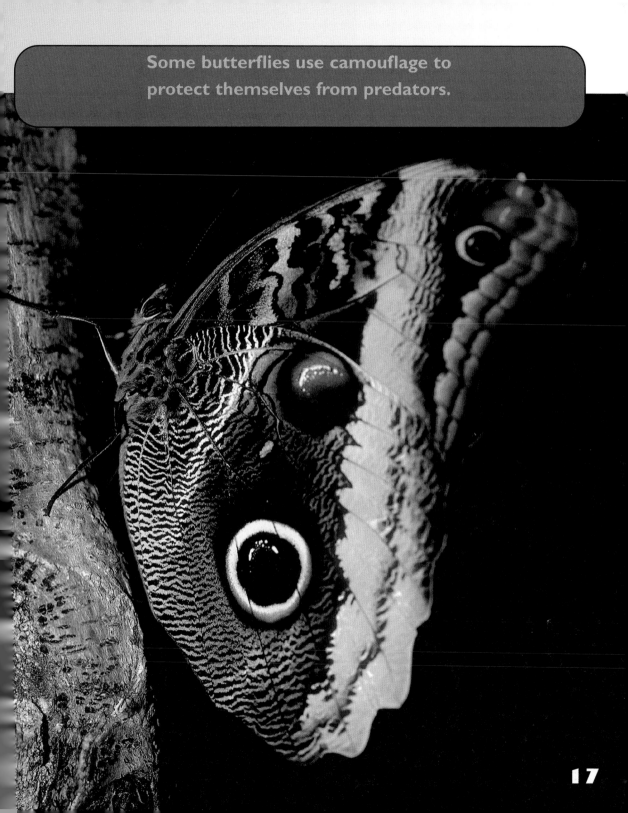

Some butterflies use camouflage to protect themselves from predators.

17

Katydids are insects that resemble grasshoppers. They both have long, thin back legs that help them jump far. However, grasshoppers have short **antennae**, while katydids have antennae as long as or longer than their bodies.

Some male katydids call to female katydids by rubbing their front wings together. The noise sounds like the words "katy did, katy didn't." This is how the insect got its name.

Katydids mostly eat leaves. They can jump quickly from leaf to leaf. When green katydids stand on green leaves, the colors blend. Brown katydids look like brown leaves and twigs. Katydids like to eat at night, when they're even harder to see.

A walkingstick doesn't have wings to help it escape predators like many other insects do. It survives because it looks like a stick! Its enemies can't tell what it is when it stands still.

Walkingsticks are found in warm places all over the world. There are nearly 3,000 kinds. The most common one in the United States has long legs and a thin body that is 2 to 3 inches (5 to 8 cm) long. A walkingstick may be brown or green like the leaves it eats.

Some kinds of walkingsticks have another adaptation. When a predator tries to eat it, the walkingstick squirts a liquid from the back of its body. The liquid burns the predator's eyes and mouth and sometimes even blinds it for a time!

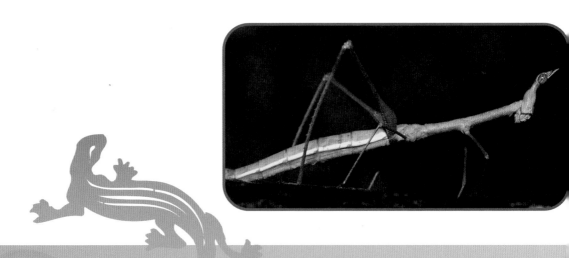

A young walkingstick can grow back
a leg if it loses one!

Camouflaged Snakes

All snakes are covered with dry scales. Underneath the outer layers are colored skin cells. Green cells help snakes hide in grass. Brown cells help snakes hide in dirt.

Some snakes have bright colors that are meant to stand out. The colors help them scare off predators. Some harmless snakes look like dangerous snakes. The coral snake is very poisonous. The scarlet kingsnake is not. Can you tell the snakes apart in the photos below?

Snakes have many other survival adaptations. Some can spread their ribs to look larger and scarier. Others can scare predators by making rattling sounds with their tails. Some can poison their enemies, while others can squeeze them to death. However, most snakes are harmless to people.

coral snake

scarlet kingsnake

This emerald tree boa waits for birds to land nearby.
It blends in with green plants.

Furry Camouflage

Polar bears are huge animals that live in the icy cold lands around the North Pole. Some grow to be 11 feet (3.4 m) long and weigh more than 1,000 pounds (454 kg)! They have two layers of thick fur to keep them warm. The outer layer of hollow hairs holds in the warmth of their bodies.

A polar bear waits near holes in the ice.
When a seal comes up for air, the bear grabs it.

Polar bear fur acts as camouflage when the bears are hunting on snow-covered land and in water. Their prey, such as seals and fish, can't see them easily in their snowy surroundings. Polar bear fur is actually colorless. It looks white because it reflects light. Underneath its fur, a polar bear's skin is black!

The arctic hare and arctic fox rely on their fur coats to protect them in their environments.

arctic hare

arctic fox

Some furry animals change colors as the seasons change. They shed their fur and grow a new coat.

Arctic foxes live around the Arctic Ocean. In the winter, they have thick white fur to match their snowy environment. In the summer, they're brown or gray to match the ground. This helps them sneak up on their prey, such as birds and small mammals.

The arctic fox hunts arctic hares. These animals also change colors as the seasons change. In the winter, arctic hares are white, and in the summer, they're brown or gray. The arctic fox and arctic hare use their camouflage to hide from each other!

arctic fox in summer

Black-and-White Camouflage

You may think that a zebra's black-and-white stripes are easy to spot. However, a zebra's stripes are actually camouflage. The stripes are mostly **vertical**, like blades of grass. Lions, the zebra's main predator, can't see colors. If a zebra stands still, its stripes help it blend in with the tall grassy plains of Africa. Lions mostly hunt at night, when a zebra's stripes make it almost impossible to see.

Zebras usually travel in large herds. This helps protect them, too. When many zebras stand together, their stripes make it hard to tell where one animal ends and another begins. A lion doesn't know where to attack.

Each zebra's stripe pattern is different.
No two patterns are exactly the same.

All Kinds of Camouflage

Animal	Color	Shape	How It Acts
reef stonefish	X	X	
nudibranch	X		
leafy sea dragon	X	X	X
ruffed grouse	X		
American bittern	X	X	X
owl butterfly	X		
katydid	X	X	
walkingstick	X	X	X
scarlet kingsnake	X		
emerald tree boa	X		
polar bear	X		
arctic fox	X		
arctic hare	X		
zebra	X		X

Glossary

adaptation (aa-dap-TAY-shun) An animal part or action that helps it stay alive.

antenna (an-TEH-nuh) A thin, rodlike feeler located on the heads of certain animals. The plural is "antennae."

crustacean (kruhs-TAY-shun) An animal that has no backbone, has a hard shell, and lives mostly in water.

environment (en-VY-ruhn-muhnt) All the living things and conditions in a place.

pigment (PIHG-muhnt) The matter in a plant or animal that gives it color.

plankton (PLANK-tuhn) Very tiny plants and animals that drift with water currents.

predator (PREH-duh-tuhr) An animal that hunts other animals for food.

reef (REEF) A strip of rocks, sand, or coral near the surface of the water.

slug (SLUHG) A slimy, snail-like animal without a shell.

snout (SNOUT) The long nose of an animal.

survive (suhr-VYV) To stay alive.

vertical (VUHR-tih-kuhl) In an up-and-down direction.

wetland (WEHT-land) An area of land where the soil is filled with or covered by water.

Index

Due to the changing nature of Internet links, The Rosen Publishing Group, Inc., has developed an online list of Web sites related to the subject of this book. This site is updated regularly. Please use this link to access the list: http://www.rcbmlinks.com/rlr/camou